TARNI'S Chance

PAUL COLLINS
JULES OBER

Sometimes, when things were bad,
Tarni retreated inside her bubble.

Then, one night, her mother whispered goodbye.

But her mother didn't come back.

One morning, Tarni woke to hear rumbling.

A garbage truck hissed and squealed as it lumbered down her street.

Suddenly, Tarni saw a dog.

She had no time to think. She flung open the door and ran.

'Look out!' she cried.

Tarni's heart thumped.
'Here, boy,' she called. 'Don't be afraid.'

Tarni felt more and more alone.

Tarni felt the dog's strong, rough coat.
'I think I'll call you Chance,' she whispered.

After school, her new friend was waiting.

'Come on, Chance . . .'

'Let's play!'

First published in 2022 by Ford Street Publishing, Melbourne, Victoria, Australia

2 4 6 8 10 9 7 5 3 1

This publication is copyright. Apart from any use as permitted under the Copyright Act 1968, no part may be reproduced by any process without prior written permission from the publisher. Requests and enquiries concerning reproduction should be addressed to Ford Street Publishing Pty Ltd, 162 Hoddle Street, Abbotsford, Vic 3067, Australia

Text copyright © Paul Collins 2022
Illustrations copyright © Jules Ober 2022
Illustrations created with resin figurines in miniature cardboard sets, photography, then post-production in Photoshop.

ISBN: 978-1-922696-05-2 HB
ISBN: 978-1-922696-06-9 PB

Printed in China by Tingleman Pty Ltd
Images by Jules Ober
Design by Joanne Marchese

www.fordstreetpublishing.com

Thanks to:

Dean Delandre for allowing the use of his painting 'Nasturtiums' in Tarni's room

Nan McNab for her patience and dedication as an editor

Pierre-Jacques Ober for his contribution to model painting and set building

the graffiti artists of Melbourne – JO.

 A catalogue record for this book is available from the National Library of Australia